D1252443

OCEANS ALIVE

Penguins

by Anne Wendorff

BLASTOFF!
2
READERS

BELLWETHER MEDIA • MINNEAPOLIS, MN

Note to Librarians, Teachers, and Parents:

Blastoff! Readers are carefully developed by literacy experts and combine standards-based content with developmentally appropriate text.

Level 1 provides the most support through repetition of high-frequency words, light text, predictable sentence patterns, and strong visual support.

Level 2 offers early readers a bit more challenge through varied simple sentences, increased text load, and less repetition of high-frequency words.

Level 3 advances early-fluent readers toward fluency through increased text and concept load, less reliance on visuals, longer sentences, and more literary language.

Level 4 builds reading stamina by providing more text per page, increased use of punctuation, greater variation in sentence patterns, and increasingly challenging vocabulary.

Level 5 encourages children to move from "learning to read" to "reading to learn" by providing even more text, varied writing styles, and less familiar topics.

Whichever book is right for your reader, Blastoff! Readers are the perfect books to build confidence and encourage a love of reading that will last a lifetime!

This edition first published in 2009 by Bellwether Media.

No part of this publication may be reproduced in whole or in part without written permission of the publisher. For information regarding permission, write to Bellwether Media Inc., Attention: Permissions Department, Post Office Box 19349, Minneapolis, MN 55419.

Library of Congress Cataloging-in-Publication Data
Wendorff, Anne.
  Penguins / by Anne Wendorff.
    p. cm. – (Blastoff! readers. Oceans alive)
  Summary: "Simple text and full color photographs introduce beginning readers to penguins. Developed by literacy experts for students in kindergarten through third grade"–Provided by publisher.
  Includes bibliographical references and index.
  ISBN-13: 978-1-60014-206-2 (hardcover : alk. paper)
  ISBN-10: 1-60014-206-0 (hardcover : alk. paper)
  1. Penguins–Juvenile literature. I. Title.
  QL696.S473W44 2009
  598.47–dc22   2008017347

Contents

Penguins are **flightless birds**. They live on land and in the ocean.

They spend as much time
in the ocean as they do
on land.

Most penguins live
around **Antarctica**.

Some penguins live on warm islands.

A penguin's body is shaped like an egg. Penguins have two wings and **webbed feet**.

8

Penguins move their wings
and webbed feet to swim.

Penguins cannot breathe underwater. They must swim to the surface for air.

beak

Penguins have beaks. They use their beaks to catch food.

Penguins hunt for food in the ocean. They eat small fish, squid, and **krill**.

Some animals hunt penguins. The colors of a penguin's feathers help them hide from **predators**.

13

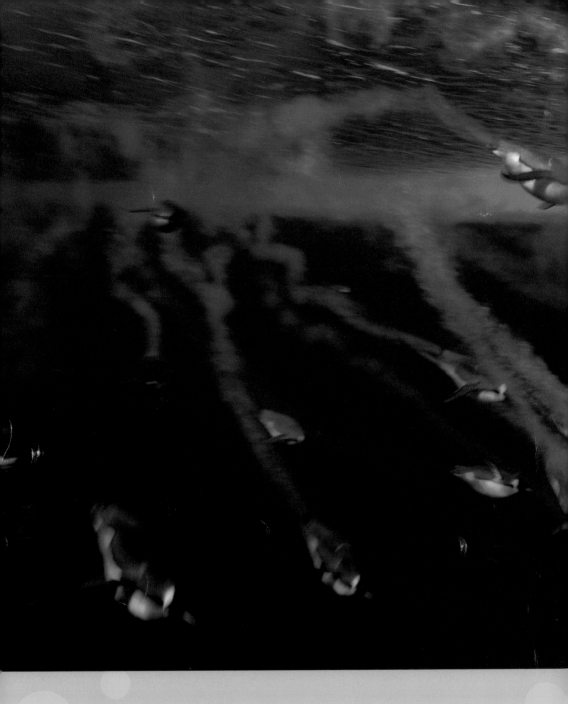

Black feathers make penguins
hard to spot for predators
flying above them.

White feathers make penguins
hard to see for predators
swimming below them.

Penguins can leap out of
the water onto land.

Penguins stand upright on land. They move with short steps or hops.

Penguins can also travel by **tobogganing**.

Penguins toboggan by sliding over the ice on their stomachs.

Some penguins stand together to keep warm.

Penguins work and play in groups. They are friendly and **social** birds.

Glossary

Antarctica—a large island covered with ice at the South Pole; some penguins live on Antarctica.

flightless bird—a kind of bird that cannot fly

krill—a small, shrimp-like animal; krill are a main source of food for penguins.

predator—an animal that hunts other animals for food; sea lions, sharks, birds, and orcas are all predators who hunt penguins.

social—living together with others in a group

tobogganing—the way penguins travel and play by sliding across ice on their stomachs

webbed feet—feet with toes connected by skin

To Learn More

AT THE LIBRARY
Black, Sonia. *Plenty of Penguins*. New York: Scholastic, 2000.

Kalman, Bobby, and Robin Johnson. *The Life Cycle of an Emperor Penguin*. New York: Crabtree, 2006.

Mitton, Tony. *Playful Little Penguins*. New York: Walker and Company, 2007.

ON THE WEB
Learning more about penguins is as easy as 1, 2, 3.

1. Go to www.factsurfer.com

2. Enter "penguins" into search box.

3. Click the "Surf" button and you will see a list of related web sites.

With factsurfer.com, finding more information is just a click away.

Index

The images in this book are reproduced through the courtesy of: Jan Martin Will, front cover; John Eastcott And Yva Momatiuk / Getty Images, pp. 4-5; Colin Moneath/ Hedgehog House / Getty Images, p. 6; Eric Gevaert, p. 7; Christian Musat, pp. 8-9; Frank Krahmer / Getty Images, p. 10; Malcolm Schuyl / Alamy, p. 11; Tui De Roy / Getty Images, p. 12; Paul Nicklen / Getty Images, p. 13; Norbert Wu / Getty Images, pp. 14-15, 16; Laitr Keiows, p. 17; Wolfgang Kaehler / Alamy, p. 18; National Geographic / Getty Images, p. 19; Daisy Gilardini / Getty Images, p. 20; Thorsten Milse / Getty Images, p. 21.